A Bumpy Ride

by Rory Thomas
illustrated by Jane Kendall

MODERN CURRICULUM PRESS
Pearson Learning Group

This is Annie Taylor.
That is Niagara Falls behind her.
Here Annie is standing on the deck of a ship.

But Annie didn't want to see the falls from a ship.

She wanted to ride over Niagara Falls in a barrel.

The falls were very high.
There were lots of rocks.

"Of course, I will need a strong barrel," said Annie.

Annie went to a man who made barrels.

"I need a strong barrel," she said. "Can you make a copy of the barrel in this picture?"

"Yes," said the man.

"Of course, I will need help," said Annie.

"We will help," said Frank and Fred.

There was no dock. But Frank stood on a rock. He took out his camera. Then he took a picture of Annie and her barrel.

Annie got into the barrel.

"Of course, I will need some air," said Annie.

Frank put air into the barrel.

Fred pushed the barrel into the river.

"I hope she steers clear of the rocks!" said Fred.

The barrel went down the river.

The barrel fell over the falls.
It hit the rocks.

The barrel was strong. It did not break.

But what about Annie?

Annie was strong too. Frank and Fred were glad. And they were proud of Annie—the first woman to go over Niagara Falls!